A New True Book

ROCKY MOUNTAIN

NATIONAL PARK

By David Petersen

CHILDRENS PRESS®
CHICAGO

Big Thompson River,
Rocky Mountain National Park

Project Editor: Fran Dyra
Design: Margrit Fiddle

Library of Congress Cataloging-in-Publication Data

Petersen, David.
    Rocky Mountain National Park / by David Petersen.
        p.   cm. — (A New true book)
    Includes index.
    Summary: Describes the landscape and wildlife of
Rocky Mountain National Park, created in 1915 and
featuring mountains, rivers, lakes, and tundra.
    ISBN 0-516-01196-0
    1.   Rocky Mountain National Park (Colo.)—Juvenile
literature.   [1.   Rocky Mountain National Park (Colo.)
2.   National parks and reserves.]   I.   Title.
F782.R59P47   1993
978.8'69—dc20   93-798
                                       CIP
                                       AC

PHOTO CREDITS

© Reinhard Brucker—2, 5, 8, 16 (2
photos), 17 (left), 21, 26 (left), 34, 37, 40
© Cameramann International, Ltd.—38
© Alan & Sandy Carey—29
H. Armstrong Roberts—© A. Bilsten,
Cover
© Jerry Hennen—32
National Park Service Photo—4, 43 (left)
Photri—© ROLOC, 19
© Branson Reynolds—11 (left), 18 (left),
25, 36, 43 (right), 44 (2 photos)
Rocky Mountain National Park — 42
(2 photos)
Root Resources—© Glenn Van
Nimwegen, 23; © Gail Nachel, 45
© James P. Rowan—27
Tom Stack & Associates—© Brian
Parker, 11 (right)
SuperStock International, Inc.—© G.
Ahrens, 6; © R.. Dahlquist, 12; © S. Vidler,
33; © The Photo Source, 39
Top Stock—© Tony Oswald, 13 (right)
Valan—© Albert Kuhnigk, 13 (left);
© Murray O'Neill, 15; © Stephen J.
Krasemann, 17 (right), 22, 30; © Michael
J. Johnson, 18 (right); © Val & Alan
Wilkinson, 26 (right)
Horizon Graphics—map on 7
COVER: Dream Lake and Hallets Peak,
Rocky Mountain National Park, Colorado

TABLE OF CONTENTS

ON TOP OF THE WORLD

Rocky Mountain National Park is in Colorado. The U.S. government made this 265,726-acre (107,535-hectare) preserve a national park in 1915.

A dedication ceremony opened Rocky Mountain National Park in 1915.

Longs Peak rises above Tyndall Creek in Rocky Mountain National Park.

"Rocky"—as its friends call it—has some of the highest and most rugged mountains in North America. It also has glaciers, rivers, lakes, and fascinating wildlife.

Trail Ridge Road crosses the high mountains in Rocky Mountain National Park.

Visiting Rocky Mountain National Park feels like being on top of the world. In fact, Rocky *is* on top of the world. Its 50-mile (80-kilometer) park highway– Trail Ridge Road–is the highest paved road in America.

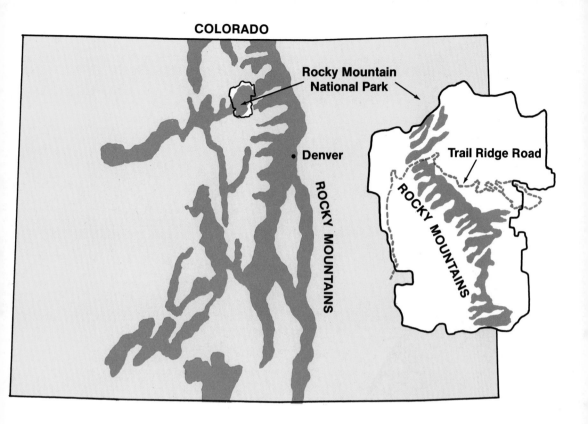

The Rocky Mountains
zigzag from north to south
down the center of the
park. Trail Ridge Road
crosses the park from east
to west, taking you over
the Rockies.

7

You can look down on the clouds from Trail Ridge Road.

At the summit, you're 12,183 feet (3,713 meters) above sea level. You can look down and see clouds *below* you!

ALPINE TUNDRA

The highest point at which trees can grow is called the timberline. Above this line, the weather is too harsh for trees. The winter is bitter cold. The winds blow at speeds of up to 200 miles (320 kilometers) per hour.

All the plants living above the timberline are very small. They must hug the ground for protection.

Up there, you can have a snowball fight on the Fourth of July!

The treeless country above the timberline is called alpine tundra. Being up on Rocky's alpine tundra is like being in the icy Arctic regions of northern Canada, Alaska, or Siberia.

Yet Rocky's tundra is full of life. Many plants that grow in Arctic regions also grow in the park. You'll

Alpine sunflower (above) and Colorado blue columbine (inset). In spring and summer, beautiful wildflowers carpet the park meadows.

see many beautiful
flowering plants there—
more than 100 species. 11

Lichens growing on a rock

You'll also see lots of fuzzy mosses and their colorful relatives—lichens. A lichen is really two tiny plants growing together—an alga and a fungus.

The pika, or "rock rabbit," lives in the

alpine zone year-round. The pika is a member of the rabbit family, but it looks more like a guinea pig.

Another alpine park animal is the marmot. Marmots are related to groundhogs. They survive

The pika (below) and the marmot (right) live on the alpine tundra.

the winter by going into underground burrows. There, they enter a deep sleep called hibernation.

Both marmots and pikas have sharp, high-pitched barks.

If you stop at one of the viewing areas along Trail Ridge Road, you may be pestered by a black, white, and gray bird called the Clark's nutcracker.

Nutcrackers belong to the crow family. They will

Clark's nutcracker

snatch food right out of
your hands if you let them.

But don't let them!
Feeding wildlife in any
national park is against the
law. It makes wild
creatures dependent on
people. Also, even a small
wild animal can give you

Male elk (above) have huge antlers that are shed in late winter. New antlers (inset) grow each summer.

a painful bite. And some animals carry dangerous diseases.

The biggest animal you're likely to see on the tundra is the elk. Elk are members of the deer family. Male elk have huge, pointed antlers.

Antlers are made of bone. They drop off, or shed, in late winter. Then during summer, they grow back again.

Up on the tundra, you'll see tiny chipmunks and

Chipmunk (left) and ground squirrel (right)

Mountain bluebird (left) and raven (right)

ground squirrels, as well as shiny black ravens and many other birds.

When you explore the alpine tundra, always stay on the trails. Tundra plants grow very slowly. Remember that a lichen you step on today could take the rest of your life to heal!

18

Stunted spruce and fir trees struggle for life in the *krummholz*.

KRUMMHOLZ

Forests of twisted little trees grow just below the timberline. This area is called the *krummholz*– German for "crooked wood."

Lower down, these same trees would be tall and straight. But near the timberline, where life is hard, the trees are stunted.

WEST ROCKY

Farther down the mountains, below the *krummholz,* the west and east sides of Rocky are two different worlds. Each side of the park gets different amounts of rain, snow, wind, and sunshine. Because of this, different kinds of plants and animals live on each side.

On the west side of the park lies the lovely Kawuneeche Valley.

The Kawuneeche Valley

Kawuneeche is an Arapaho name. It means "Coyote's Valley."

21

Coyote howling. These wolflike animals hunt small rodents.

Coyotes belong to the dog family. They look like small wolves. They get together at sunrise and sunset to yap and sing with wild joy. These "song dogs" live throughout the park.

Male moose feeding on willow brush

   The biggest animal in
Rocky is the moose.
Moose are the largest
members of the deer
family. They are as big as
a horse! Watch for these
huge, dark-brown animals
in the marshes and forests

of Kawuneeche Valley. Their favorite foods are willow brush and other marsh plants.

Because they are so big, moose can be dangerous. Always watch moose from a safe distance.

One special tree that grows in Rocky is the quaking aspen. You can recognize aspens by their smooth, white bark. Aspen leaves have long, flattened stems. These flat stems allow the leaves to

The leaves of quaking aspens turn a bright golden color in the fall.

tremble, or quake, in the
slightest breeze.

In autumn, aspen leaves
turn from green to gold.
An aspen grove in fall is
a beautiful sight.

Beavers (inset) live in lodges built of mud and tree branches.

The beaver is a large rodent that lives in the water and eats aspen twigs and bark. Look for the wood-and-mud beaver dams and lodges along the streams in

Kawuneeche Valley.

The Colorado River runs through
the western part of the park.

On the west side of the
park are the headwaters—
or beginnings—of the
mighty Colorado River.

The Colorado River
begins as hundreds of tiny
streams made by melting

snow. As these streams join, the main channel gets larger and larger. Finally it becomes a river.

From the park, the Colorado snakes south and west through Utah. It then flows through Arizona's Grand Canyon. After a voyage of 1,400 miles (2,253 kilometers), this great river, which began as melting snow high in Colorado, empties into the Gulf of California.

EAST ROCKY

The east side of the park is much drier. You won't see any moose there. They prefer wet, marshy areas.

But the east side of Rocky has a big animal too. And you won't see it on the west side. It's the Rocky Mountain bighorn sheep. Just call it "bighorn."

Rocky Mountain bighorn sheep

Bighorn sheep
live in
groups of up to
sixty animals.

Only male moose and
elk grow antlers. But both
male and female sheep
grow horns. However, the

horns of the male sheep are much larger than those of the female.

Another difference between horns and antlers is that horns aren't shed and regrown each year the way antlers are. Instead, the same set of horns continues to grow throughout a bighorn's life.

The best place in Rocky Mountain National Park for watching bighorn sheep is Horseshoe Park, near Sheep Lakes. Bighorns

Bighorn sheep at a mineral lick

come to Horseshoe Park
for its mineral licks. A
mineral lick is a place
where salt, iron, and other
natural minerals are present
in the soil or water.

For a bighorn, eating the
soil and drinking the
muddy water at a mineral
lick is like taking vitamin

pills. It provides the animal
with important nutrients.

From the mountain
tundra of the Mummy
Range, the bighorns come

The Mummy Range of mountains is in the northern part of the park.

Sheep Lakes in Horseshoe Park

down to the mineral licks
at Horseshoe Park almost
every day.

On their way into the
meadow, the sheep cross
the park road. To protect
the bighorns—and the

motorists—park rangers stop traffic while the sheep are crossing the road.

When you come to see Rocky Mountain National Park's bighorn sheep, be sure to bring your binoculars and camera.

In addition to its fascinating wildlife, the east side of Rocky has glaciers. A glacier is a huge mass of ice. Glaciers are formed when more snow falls every winter

Andrews Glacier is one of the park's many mountain glaciers.

than can melt during the summers.

Glaciers are always moving—sliding s-l-o-w-l-y down mountain valleys.

They are like rivers of ice.

Snowcapped mountains are mirrored in Mills Lake.

THREE PARKS IN ONE

As you can see, Rocky is really three parks in one: the alpine tundra, the damp west side, and the drier east side.

37

Camping trailer and tent in one of Rocky's many campgrounds

After you have explored the tundra, *krummholz,* and lower elevations, and watched the wildlife, what else is there to do at Rocky? Plenty!

Rocky has campgrounds, picnic areas, horseback

riding, and trout fishing.
And there are more than
350 miles (563 kilometers)
of hiking trails.

The park has at least
150 lakes and many

A view of Bear Lake

beautiful waterfalls. There are five visitor centers. In addition to all that, Rocky has one of the best museums anywhere.

The theme of the Moraine Park Museum is "The Making of a Landscape." The exhibits tell about the park's plants, animals, weather, history, and geology. Geology is the study of the earth's natural features.

Opposite page: Alberta Falls is one of Rocky's many beautiful waterfalls.

Displays at Moraine Park Museum

Moraine Park Museum has "living" displays that show how geology works. For example, these displays allow you to build mountains and rip them apart, or slide glaciers down the mountains.

Young visitors attend a "ranger talk" at Rocky
to help them earn a Junior Ranger badge.

Ask at the museum about becoming a Rocky's Junior Ranger. You can earn an official Junior Ranger badge in three easy steps. Complete the "Rocky's Rookie Rangers" workbook, pick up ten pieces of litter, and take part in one ranger-led activity.

Glacier Gorge was carved by moving rivers of ice. A sign
(inset) explains how glaciers formed the landscape.

There are so many fun
things to see and do at
Rocky Mountain National
Park. A visit there will
surely have you feeling
"on top of the world."

WORDS YOU SHOULD KNOW

alga (AL • ga) — a tiny plant that can make its own food

alpine (AL • pyne) — like high mountains; growing or living in high mountains

antlers (ANT • lerz) — a bony, hornlike growth on the head of an animal such as an elk or a moose

Arapaho (ah • RAP • ah • hoe) — a group of Native Americans who once lived in Colorado

Arctic (ARK • tik) — the cold and icy region of the world around the North Pole

burrow (BER • oh) — a hole, or tunnel, in the ground

channel (CHAN • il) — the bed of a river or a stream

coyote (ky • OH • tee) — a wild animal that looks like a small wolf

display (dis • PLAY) — objects set up to show how they work or to explain how they relate to each other

elevation (el • ih • VAY • shun) — height

exploring (ex • PLORE • ing) — traveling to look at one's surroundings and to find new things

fungus (FUNG • us) — a plant that has no flowers or leaves and no green coloring

geology (gee • AH • luh • gee) — the study of the earth's features and history

glacier (GLAY • sher) — a thick mass of snow and ice that moves slowly across land or down a mountain

grove (GROHVE) — a group of trees of the same kind growing close together

guinea pig (GINN • ee PIG) — a small rodent with short ears and a short tail

headwaters (HED • wah • terz) — the place where a river or stream begins

hibernation (hie • ber • NAY • shun) — a state of deep sleep in which body temperature drops and breathing slows

krummholz (KRUM • holts) — an area of small, twisted trees

lichen (LY • kin) — an alga and a fungus growing together

litter (LIH • ter) — trash; garbage

marsh (MARSH) — a low area of land covered with shallow water and rich in plant life

meadow (MEH • dow) — a grassy area with few trees

mineral lick (MIN • ril LIK) — a place where minerals that animals need for health are present in the soil or water

museum (myoo • ZEE • um) — a place where interesting objects are collected and shown

nutrients (NOO • tree • ints) — elements that are essential to keep living things strong and healthy, such as proteins, carbohydrates, fats, vitamins, and minerals

pika (PY • ka) — a small animal related to the rabbit

preserve (prih • ZERV) — an area set aside to be protected from farming, building, or other development

quaking (KWAY • king) — shaking; trembling

rodent (ROH • dint) — an animal that has long, sharp front teeth for gnawing

sea level (SEE LEH • vil) — the level of the surface of the ocean

species (SPEE • ceez) — a group of plants or animals that are of the same kind

stunted (STUN • tid) — kept from growing or developing

summit (SUM • it) — the very top of a mountain; the highest point of a road or trail that crosses a mountain range

trout (TROUT) — a tasty fish found in lakes and streams

tundra (TUN • dra) — a cold, treeless area where the plant life consists of short grasses, mosses, and lichens

INDEX

About the Author

David Petersen is a writer, teacher, and outdoorsman living in southwest Colorado.